Real Estate

Rental Property Investment Guide

How To Buy & Manage Rental Property For Profits

Introduction

This book has actionable information on how to buy and manage rental property for steady passive income and financial freedom.

Rental properties; they certainly seem like a lucrative passive income opportunity because they offer one of the basic needs of us humans; shelter. As such, the market for rental properties seems to be guaranteed compared to many other forms of businesses, which have some chances of failure. Think about it; when you have a rental property, you are more or less guaranteed an income whether or not you work. This makes rental properties some of the best investment vehicles for any age because even at old age, when you may not have all the energy to pursue active income businesses, your rental property will still bring rental income. This probably explains why so many [millionaires have invested in real estate](). That's definitely a cool idea. Well, despite the allure of easy money that comes with rental properties, you need much more than just doing the bare minimum if you truly want to excel while at it.

Despite the fact that rental properties share many similarities with property for outright sale, only the most naïve and unassuming would consider them the same. Certainly, some things remain similar across the board; for instance, whether you own a rental property or property for sale, you will need to maintain and manage your property in a similar manner.

However, rental houses are a different bag of beans. *Before you make the decision to buy a property for rental purposes (before you decide to become a property owner), you have to consider a number of things.*

For instance, *you have to consider the property location i.e. the social amenities in close proximity; the tenant age group you are targeting (you will have to deal with tenants, some of whom will hold your property with little regard as far as taking care of the property is concerned) and for as long as you own that property, you will have to cover maintenance costs.*

Thus, although an excellent way to earn a passive ***income, before you dive feet first into the rental property business, you need to understand what you are getting yourself into, which is what this book attempts to help you do***.

As you venture into buying and managing rental real estate properties, you need to make sound choices from the word go; make the perfect purchase, make the perfect management choices, offer perfect rental charges, etc. This book shall show you how to do these things and so much more. In this book, you will learn:

- ***Valuable insights that will help you start investing in rental property from a point of knowledge***
- ***How to search and analyze rental properties like a pro***
- ***Rental property math that you need to master to ensure you maximize your returns and don't get burned***
- ***14 critical steps and measures you should take to manage your rental property optimally***
- ***How to decide between working with a property manager or managing your property by yourself***
- ***And much, much more!***

If you want to learn all that, **download this book NOW!** You will never regret it! You will thank me later!

I hope you enjoy it!

PS: I'd like your feedback. If you are happy with this book, please leave a review on Amazon.

Please leave a review for this book on Amazon by visiting the page below:

https://amzn.to/2VMR5qr

Table of Contents

Introduction 2

Easing You In: Your Rental Property Knowledge Bank 12

    1: Property Taxes Will Be High 13

    2: Tenants may cause far much more damage than you may expect 14

    3: You'd better make a haven for your good tenants 15

    4: The cost of repairs is unreasonably high and unexpected 15

    5: Rules must be there and must be followed 16

Value for Money: How to Search, and Analyze Rental Properties 18

    1: The Neighborhood 18

    2: The Property Taxes 19

3: Schools 19

4: Crime Levels...20

5: The Job Market 21

6: Amenities 21

7: Building Permits and Future Development 22

8: The Number of Listings and Vacancies...........22

Analysis and Comparison: A Comprehensive Coverage of Rental Properties Calculations and Computations 24

Cap Rate 24

The Intuition Behind (& Importance Of) the Cap Rate 26

When and When You Should Not Use Cap Rate . 27

The Down Payment and Rate of Interest 29

Property Tax..30

Homeowners Insurance 31

Maintenance 31

Utilities 32

Tenant Search 32

The 14 Most Critical Steps and Measures for Optimum Rental Property Management 34

1: Emotional Management 34

2: Put In Place A Maintenance and Repair System 35

3: Always Overestimate Repair and Maintenance Costs 35

4: Marketing and Advertising Is Costly: Plan Meticulously 36

5: Plan for Bloated Property Taxes 36

6: Prepare For Rental Charge Declines 36

7: The "Rental Property Glut" Is Real: Anticipate It 37

8: On Race, Ethnicity, Sex, Religion and Other Unique Traits 37

9: Plan on Having "Reserves" 38

10: The "2 Month Rent Dissipation" 38

11: Keep Sentiments and Emotions at Bay 38

12: Managing the Control Factor 38

13: Think Long Term 39

14: Internalize Your State's Landlord-Tenant Laws 39

Property Manager or A Property Management Company VS Self-Managing 40

When to Consider Hiring a Property Management Company 40

The Responsibilities of a Property Manager/Property Management Firm 41

Scenarios That Should Move You to Hire Such a Company 42

Conclusion 45

© Copyright 2018 by Fantonpublishers.com - All rights reserved.

Before you can learn how to make the most from rental property, it is important to have an in-depth understanding about rental properties. That's where we will begin.

Easing You In: Your Rental Property Knowledge Bank

Owning rental properties offers you the chance to earn a substantial passive income that covers the mortgage price, as well as the maintenance costs you will have to deal with at some point. Additionally, rentals allow you to pay off all these costs using the tenants' money as opposed to your own.

However, buying and managing rentals is not a painless ride. While this chapter will cover some of the most important experiences you should insulate yourself against, you will have to learn a few things the hard way: by getting started on the business and learning as you go along.

Here are some things you should know before you venture into the field; many rental property owners wish they had known these things before they spent a penny on rentals:

1: Property Taxes Will Be High

You may not know this, but in most US states, the tax caps on rental property are a full percentage higher than your primary residence or on regular homesteads. What does this mean for you? Perhaps, the best way to explain it is to give a real example:

"I will never forget the first day I opened my property tax bill. It was the rudest shock I had in a long time. My property taxes had gone up at least 300%. I mean; I knew that the taxes had to go up somewhat but the rate at which they went up with was not something I had expected to happen." - Carol- Rental property owner

Usually, the problem will arise if you base your rental price on your old mortgage bill and not the new one. This is how a bloated property tax bill surprises you. For the first year after you rent your property, you may sway between broke and "just adrift". How do you solve this?

Well, given that this book is already giving you an early warning, you need not wait until the first year's rental lease ends to adjust your rent prices. You need to start with the right price- a price that is not too high for the tenant or too low to a point where it cannot cover your property tax costs.

If you ignore the advice here, like Carol, you will learn this lesson the hard way.

2: Tenants may cause far much more damage than you may expect

If you have a conversation with any seasoned rental property owner, you will probably hear a horror story or two of horrific damages left behind by former tenants. Here is the thing- you do know that these things may happen. However, as is the case with most newbie owners, you may envision being on the receiving end of it.

The reality is that at one point or another, you will have to deal with some considerable damage especially if you are dealing with tenants that have teenage children; it is often a matter of when, not if, damage to property will occur especially if the parents are often away at work.

If you pick the windows as the likeliest to suffer damage, you are right. If you stop there, you may be in for a rude shock. Have you provided a carpet in the house? Tenants use "Free" carpets without much regard. Some property owners have reported missing doors or doors ripped off their hinges, or previously intact doors now supported by a combination of nails and rubber. The lesson here is to expect anything. It is highly unlikely that every tenant you house will hold your property in as high a regard as you do.

3: You'd better make a haven for your good tenants

In as much as some tenants utterly disregard rentals, other tenants are the exact opposite. You likely know the kind and may have come across them at some point in your life. Perhaps in your rent paying days, you were one such tenant. These tenants will take care of the home as if it was their home.

They will decorate when the festivities come around and will keep the lawn neat and tidy. Often, these tenants have little need for constant movement. If you have tenants like these, treat them with all the consideration in the world. Do not whimsically raise rent fees. These types of tenants are rare and hard to come across.

4: The cost of repairs is unreasonably high and unexpected

If you aim to furnish your rental to some degree, you can expect to replace a furnace at some point, an air conditioner or two, a refrigerator more than once and a stove. You can expect to pay for a new sump pump and underwater draining system down the line.

You will spend hundreds of dollars on drywall repairs, fresh coats of paint and carpeting. All these repairs are age related as opposed to carelessness on the tenants' part: you are yet to factor in the repairs you will have to handle in the case of irresponsible tenants.

The fortunate part is that most of these funds will come from the pockets of the renters. Still, you can expect that some of the money you spend will come directly from your own pocket especially in your first year.

5: Rules must be there and must be followed

Do you know the worst crime you can commit as a property owner? Well, as a proprietor, the worst crime you can commit is to be non-confrontational. It is okay to set rules and insist on their adherence.

Often, you will need to put your foot down on rent paying. If you are too nice and allow the tenants to "pay when they can," do not be surprised if they insist on "paying when they can" for the next two years.

Here is the deal: as a property owner, even if you enjoy mutual friendship and admiration for each tenant, the first thing your tenant is to you is your tenant. If you have rules that stipulate a 10-dollar fine for every day the rent is late, do not shirk enforcing it.

Now that you know some of the things you should prepare for, let us look at how to search for, and analyze rental properties before you make a purchase.

Value for Money: How to Search, and Analyze Rental Properties

This section of the guide will look at some of the most vital things to consider when searching for the right property. Your analysis should be thorough. Replace your sentiment with intense analyzing and you will do fine (the next section will cover smart calculations you need to do when looking for the perfect property).

Here are the things you should consider:

1: The Neighborhood

The type and quality of neighborhood you choose will influence the kind of tenants you attract as well as how often you deal with vacancies. Take the example of a neighborhood located near a university. Such a rental property will attract university students. While your prices may have to be relatively low to accommodate students, you will most likely have a healthy traffic of renters. However, you can also expect occasional vacancies such as during holidays when students tend to home.

2: The Property Taxes

The previous section mentions taxes, and the unique tax-cap rental properties attract. You also need to understand that property taxes are not usually standard across the board.

As a property investor looking to earn a passive income from rent money, you will want to know how much you are losing to the taxman. The truth is that high property taxes may not necessarily be a bad thing if you own property in an excellent neighborhood with a minimal rate of vacancies. The trouble is that these two do not always go hand in hand. Your town's assessment office (there is one for sure) will have all the necessary tax information on file. If this is too much work, you can always talk to the homeowners in your community.

3: Schools

If you are targeting couples as the ideal tenants, you can bet that children may be on the agenda and that they will be looking for property with a nearby school. When you find good property near a school, your first step should be to find out the reputation and quality of the school.

What does a school have to do with your property? Well, the quality of the school will directly influence the value of your property. If the school's reputation is poor, your investment will also be poor in value, which will make it hard to justify your prices even if they are reasonable. Even if this is not the case, if you do decide to sell your property at some time, your projected value and the projected value of your potential buyers will be dissimilar.

4: Crime Levels

Few people will fancy living next door to a crime hotspot. Even testosterone junkies prefer their roughhousing served at the confines of bars. Take your time and visit the public library or the police station for accurate stats on crime rates. Asking the man/woman selling you the property about it is lazy and ill informed. Why would he/she jeopardize the sale by telling you anything other than what you would want to hear?

Here are some things to check: serious crimes, rates of vandalism, petty crimes, and the most recent crime activity (slow down or growth). You may also consider asking police frequency in the neighborhood.

5: The Job Market

Locations that boast growing employment opportunities will tend to attract more people and more tenants. There is a way to find out how a neighborhood rates on this one. Go straight to the U.S Bureau of Labor Statistics or the local library.

If you hear of a new company moving into the area, your smart money will be on potential workers flooding in. Sure enough, this will negatively or positively reflect on the house prices. The former is most likely. Nevertheless, here is your fallback: as a smart investor, figuratively speaking, you will want the new corporation to be in your backyard.

6: Amenities

Check your potential neighborhood for current parks or any projected ones. Check for malls, gyms, public transport hubs, movie theatres, and other amenities that will attract tenants. Most cities will have promotional literature that gives you an idea of where the ideal blend of amenities and private property merge.

7: Building Permits and Future Development

The municipal planning department will usually have all the information you need on new developments coming into your area of interest. If you notice new condominiums, malls, and business parks cropping up in the area, it is a sign that the area is a good growth area.

However, before jumping in feet first, it will be smart to look out for any new developments, which could actually end up hurting your investment or the surrounding property pricing. For instance, is there a new development that will, in the end, cause the loss of friendly green space?

What about those additional condominiums coming up; will they offer intense competition for your renters? The idea here is to target an area that shows signs of healthy growth but at the same time, determine if the healthy growth is healthy for your investment.

8: The Number of Listings and Vacancies

Take this one very seriously. If the prices of the properties are unbelievably good, but when you look into it, the neighborhood shows an unusually high number of listings, perhaps this may be due to a seasonal cycle, in which case, you should not shirk from making your purchase.

However, it could also be a sign that the neighborhood has gone bad. Before you invest, determine which one it is. You should also determine your ability to cover any season-based fluctuations related to vacancies. Similar to listings, vacancies rates will give you a clear picture of how successful you are likely to be at attracting new tenants and retaining them. Here is some basic math for you: high rates of vacancies FORCE proprietors to lower rent rates in a bid to attract tenants. Low rates of vacancies ALLOW property owners to raise rent rates.

With that understanding, you probably feel excited about taking the leap to buy rental property. Before you do, you need to do some math to enable you to understand whether the investment you are making is worthwhile. We will learn how to do that in the next chapter.

Analysis and Comparison: A Comprehensive Coverage of Rental Properties Calculations and Computations

Every property owner needs to know some basic math given that some calculations will be indispensable to your business. Why is this important? Well, simply because there are many fast and loose interpretations of such formulas and mostly, those who go by them end up getting hurt.

You ought to remember that when you are buying your property, the seller is going to get a little creative to minimize expenses. You, the buyer, must apply the proper formulas to determine the buying price for your property. Here are the most important calculations and computations:

Cap Rate

The capitalization rate, known popularly as cap rate, is a fundamental concept in real estate investment yet it is one of the most widely misunderstood (and consequently, misused) concepts in commercial real estate. This sub-section will demystify the cap rate concept.

The Definition

The capitalization rate, also referred to as cap rate, is simply the ratio of NOI (Net Operating Income) to property value. For instance, if a property listing is $1,000,000 and then generated a NOI of $100,000, you could say its cap rate is 10% ($100,000/$1,000,000).

[Capitalization Rate= annual net operating income/cost (or value)]

Net Operating Income (NOI) = Gross Operating Income- expenses

This is hands down the most common metric used by investors. The seller will often drastically underrate expenses. You will need to ask for copies of original bills. If the seller refuses or acts shady about them, just move on to the next seller and apply this standard of honesty.

What Are The Expenses?

Expenses will include bills such as natural gas, water, electricity, and property tax. This calculation is also inclusive of a percentage for maintenance, vacancy allowance, and property management. Property sellers conveniently leave out some of these expenses. This will be your safety margin;

at some point, as sure as anything, you will need this safety margin.

Cap Rate Example:

Let us shed some light on how property's cap rate commonly applies.

Supposing you are researching the recent sale of a Class A office block with a Net Operating Income (NOI) of $1,000,000 and a price of $17,000,000. In the commercial world of real estate, it is common to conclude that this property "sold" at a 5.8% cap rate.

[Cap Rate= NOI/VALUE]

[Cap Rate= $1,000,000/$17,000,000]

[Cap Rate= 0.0583432]

[Cap Rate = (0.05 x 100) %]

[Cap Rate= 5.08%]

The Intuition Behind (& Importance Of) the Cap Rate

What message is the Cap Rate trying to pass across to you, the buyer? One intuitive way to think about it is that it is representative of the percentage return that any investor should expect to receive if he/she were to do an all-cash purchase.

Take the above example for instance. If you did an all-cash purchase of that property, it would mean that it would return an annual return on your investment of 5.8%. Yet another way to think about Cap Rate is that it is simply the inverse of the multiple of price/earnings.

When and When You Should Not Use Cap Rate

In commercial real estate industry, the cap rate is common and very useful. It is very helpful in different situations. For instance, it can help you quickly size up your acquisition relative to other investment properties you are also considering. For example, a 5% cap rate versus a 10% cap rate acquisition for a similar property in a similar location should instantly signal to you that one property has a loftier risk premium than its counterpart.

Another instance the cap rate can be helpful is when it forms a trend. If you are looking at the trends of cap rates over the several years within a specific sub market, then the trend may actually give you a very good indication of the direction in which particular market is heading.

For instance, if you notice steadily compressing cap rates, this shows you that properties are bidding upwards and the market is getting hotter by the year. Where are your values apt to be next year or in two years' time? Looking at the trend of cap rates will give you good insight into the direction that your valuations will take.

While cap rates are handy for swift back-of-the-envelope computations, it is vital to note when NOT to use cap rates. When you apply this to a stabilized Net Operating Income projection, the simple capitalization rate may end up producing a valuation that is approximately equal to that, which is generated using a significantly more complex DCF (Discounted Cash Flow) analysis. However, if the NOI shows characteristic complexity and irregularity with significant variations in cash flow, using cap rate will NOT give you a credible and reliable valuation.

When deciding what to offer for a property, you will want to analyze the deferred maintenance carefully both within the apartments as well as throughout the whole building.

Deferred maintenances are maintenances the previous owner should have done but skipped.

You shall also want to glean as much information as you can about the building. What was the property before its listing for sale? Was it a brothel? Was it a drug house? Was there a horrific murder in the building? Have the tenants in the building been there long? What is the general reputation of this building?

Granted, these things are outdated and should have little if any influence on how the building shapes up in future; however, like most people, tenants are sentiment driven. You must cater to it, even though you may not want to.

To gather this information, the best way is the old school way. You will need to wake up early one morning, patrol the building alone (without the estate agent) and ensure to knock around; you will know the situation on the ground much more.

The Down Payment and Rate of Interest

With rental rates constantly on the rise, rental properties have become the investor's greatest avenue. However, lenders view rental property investments as part of the "edgy" and riskier group of investments. Thus, they will ask for a minimum down payment of 20% and a 0.75% higher interest rate. If your property is a three to four unit property, the lender will only do with a minimum of 25%.

Why is this important to know? For starters, most banks and lenders hold real estate for rental purposes in different light. However, the top reason why this is important is that it allows you to choose your property not based on how much you fancy it, but depending on how much you can pay for it up front.

If you regard some rental property favorably but cannot put up at least 20% of its value (which is required by the bank, no exceptions), consider moving on to the next best property you can pay a down payment for.

Property Tax

Depending on the neighborhood, property tax may significantly add to the cost of the property. Directly contact the municipality to ensure the listed taxes on the Multiple Listing Service (MLS) are accurate. It will also be wise to find out just what services those particular services will include. For instance, is removal of garbage included?

Why is this important? As far as positive cash flow goes, how much you give up in taxes will factor in significantly. If you are estimating a positive cash flow, it is all for naught if you do not factor in taxes. More importantly, you must understand that the tax cap for rentals is usually more bloated than is usual. You need to find out what the taxable services entail so that if you deem them unnecessary, you could always eliminate them, thus reducing your tax burden. The idea is to do everything within legal confines.

Homeowners Insurance

Insurance may significantly vary depending on your region especially if your area has a reputation for flooding, fire hazards, and other perils. Before you sign anything, take your time and discuss rates with an insurance rep.

Why is this vital to weigh? Because insurance is not free- you will need to pay a price to insure your property. Because you will be using your money, especially in the first month, it is important to understand the risks in the area and by extension, how this affects what you pay as insurance money. This will help you accurately estimate positive cash flow.

Maintenance

To cover maintenance costs and the cost of having vacancies, as a rule of thumb, it is best to keep about 11-12 months of rent for every single property. This is especially applicable for the property owner who "owns a few properties" (as a novice or beginner, it is safe to assume you will start small before expanding).

It is a great idea to budget 10-15% of the annual rent for upkeep and maintenance of your property. This is in addition to any damage caused by the tenant that ought to be covered by security deposits.

Utilities

Utilities like electricity and gas are often the tenant's responsibility. However, some utilities like sewer and water may be included in the rental charge. If you intend to include such kind in the rent, get an estimate from utility companies pertaining the mean monthly usage.

Tenant Search

Finding good tenants carries some cost. A basic set up is to charge a non-refundable fee of application to prospective tenants. For instance, you could charge a $25 application fee.

This separates serious, keen, and responsible tenants from those who may not have these traits.

However, that is tricky ground to tread upon especially as a beginner. The simple solution is to hire a property manager or an agent to take care of the tenant search for you. Property managers and agents will often give you value for money. However, you will have to fork up some money for the service.

We what we have learnt on how to buy rental property in mind, let's move on to the next bit, which is a guide on how to manage rental property.

The 14 Most Critical Steps and Measures for Optimum Rental Property Management

The previous sections have placed emphasis on helping you select and purchase the ideal rental investment property. You shall also be glad to know that with the dip in real estate prices, if you act fast, you can have good property at some of the best prices possible.

Prices have dipped so much that the concept of positive cash flow on rental houses is a firm reality. However, before you leap into the deep end (and it sure is deep), consider the following self-management tips that property owners with vast experience have drawn up.

1: Emotional Management

Being a proprietor is incredibly tough. You will have to deal with deadbeat tenants, late paying tenants, evictions, repairs, and other maintenances. If you are not emotionally primed to deal with these issues, you will not succeed. Look at it this way; when the toilet is not flushing properly, or there is a bit of a snag in the air conditioning, to your tenant, this is an emergency needing immediate attendance. Do you know whom your tenants will be calling? That is right- you. Expect rude interruptions in the middle of important business meetings and family get-togethers.

2: Put In Place A Maintenance and Repair System

Occasionally, you will have to deal with several repair and maintenance issues. Without such a system, it will be difficult to get on top of such scenarios. A maintenance and repair system will enable swift and effective action. However, on its own, it will not be enough. You will need to have a handy repairperson one call away, a competent plumber, and Air Conditioning Corporation, a roofer and an electrician.

3: Always Overestimate Repair and Maintenance Costs

Repairs and maintenance may very well end up costing you a lot more than anticipated. What is more; every time you have to eject a deadbeat tenant, it falls on your shoulders to make the space rentable.

Cleaning up is only the base activity- a lot of the time, you will have to repaint the place, replace carpeting and windows, and so forth. Not only will this require money, rental charges will not offset these costs.

4: Marketing and Advertising Is Costly: Plan Meticulously

Marketing and advertising can be very expensive. Expect to pay for ads, lock boxes, signs, flyers, and the like.

5: Plan for Bloated Property Taxes

After you invest in a property and mark it down as rental property, expect a significant rise in property taxes and insurance rates. Understand this: in the first year, things may be tough. However, when you get past the first yearly lease and make enough modifications to warrant an increase in rental charges, it gets better.

6: Prepare For Rental Charge Declines

Property owners forced to lower rental prices is common. This could be because of any number of reasons. Perhaps, the competition has become fiercer or there is steady movement of tenants from your neighborhood to another one. With this in mind, understand that negative cash flow situations are a reality, especially when the combination of high payments and low rental charges is in place.

7: The "Rental Property Glut" Is Real: Anticipate It

What is this glut? Well, rental property glut is a rental situation that has come about because of "unwilling" proprietors. Here is a simpler explanation: with the foreclosure crisis looming and a scarcity of buyers willing to buy the property, sellers who have little success making an outright sale revert to renting out the property. This brings about a glut of rental properties. In America, this is a very real thing and while it has been very favorable for tenants, it has been cruel on property owners. Understand that it may take several years before this glut clears out.

8: On Race, Ethnicity, Sex, Religion and Other Unique Traits

There is no middle ground on this one: when renting out, do not discriminate. Doing so is tantamount to violating Federal Housing Laws. Look out for local laws too, with the inclusion of code enforcement requirements and zoning.

9: Plan on Having "Reserves"

You should have up to six month's reserves in case you have to deal with emergencies such as damaged roofs, floods, hurricanes, and so forth.

10: The "2 Month Rent Dissipation"

When you calculate cash flow, always assume that a month's rent will channel to handling repairs and another month's rent will cover vacancies. This is conservative, but it is a very wise assumption. It considers that you will have 10 months' rent out of twelve for every calendar year.

11: Keep Sentiments and Emotions at Bay

Being a property owner is a business: if you treat it as anything other than this, you will hurt your cash flow. Being sentimental is folly. Your tenants' rental payment is what pays your mortgage- if they cannot pay, they have to leave by choice or forceful eviction.

12: Managing the Control Factor

In rental investment, there is a short rule: either you control your tenant or he/she controls you. You need to be firm with those who are not prompt with payments. If you deem it necessary, pin a three-day notice on the door. Make your tenants understand that late payments are intolerable; doing this may very well determine your success as a proprietor.

13: Think Long Term

The truest real estate sentence there ever was supports this. No property owner has ever become rich over the short term. It takes considerable time for real estate appreciation.

14: Internalize Your State's Landlord-Tenant Laws

For example, Florida is a very proprietor friendly state. New York on the other hand handles tenants with kid's gloves. Carefully consider where you aim to invest, and the landlord-tenant laws of that state.

Now that you have a good understanding of important things you should know when managing rental property, the next thing you may want to ask yourself is; are you going to self manage or use the services of a management company? Let's learn how to make that decision in the next chapter.

Property Manager or A Property Management Company VS Self-Managing

As a rental real estate property owner, one of the things you should consider is whether you should personally manage your properties or hire a property manager or property management company to do it for you.

When to Consider Hiring a Property Management Company

As a property owner, one of the bigger decisions you will have in your hands is whether to hire a property managing company or not. In truth, this can be a good or bad move for your business. Sometimes though, you will need help managing your property. This will be clear for you to see as a rational businessperson. When you notice considerable strain on your self-managing efforts, it makes sense to hire someone to manage your property.

Such companies may end up shaping up into your property's greatest asset. The catch is that the services of these companies never come cheap. You also may have other reasons why you cannot hire one. Mull over the decision and weigh the factors discussed in the ensuing paragraphs to determine if hiring a second party to manage your property is a good move.

The Responsibilities of a Property Manager/Property Management Firm

These companies/individuals will act as a buffer between you and tenants and prospects. Rather than having to deal with them and chase some down, the company will handle them directly. This may lift off a lot of stress: you will not have to fuss over the condition of your rentals, slack rental pay, repair issues, handling maintenance, responding to complaints and tenant eviction.

In addition to this, a good management company will inject knowledge and intelligent activity in your property. This will have the effect of giving you a peaceful mind because you understand that your property is in competent hands.

On a final note, such companies are independent contractors. This will save you the hassle that comes with having to take an employer's stance over them.

Scenarios That Should Move You to Hire Such a Company

Hiring someone or a company to help you manage your rental properties is ideal when:

1. You have many rental units: The more rental properties you own, the more units they will have. Thus, you will benefit from having a management company handling your affairs.

2. You live a considerable distance away from your property: If you live a distance away from your rental property, hiring a company to take care of management will greatly benefit you since it will take care of issues that may be hard handle from a distance.

3. You have no interest in hands-on management: Hands-on management, or the idea of it, is not everyone's cup of tea. While some landlords look forward to the challenge that finding good tenants brings, if you view the ownership of rental property as an investment that needs handling in an impersonal way, consider hiring such a company.

4. You have time constraints: You may enjoy the thrill that comes with self-managing your property but have very little time to dedicate to it. This is especially so if you have a day job. The other scenario is where you dedicate your time to expansion activity such as finding new properties, arranging for financing and renovations, or altering your business structure. If this is your case, consider hiring such a company.

5. You can handle the cost without much hassle: Hiring a company or someone to manage your property will be an attractive option to exercise if you have the resources for it.

When looking to hire a company, expect quotations of anything from 5% to 10% of collected rent. If it is a down market and it is within your capacity to manage things on your own, it may be smart to keep things as they are until the market swings around.

6. There is a sudden influx of management tasks: If your business is recording steady growth, with time, you may need help to manage everything in proper form. At this point, consider hiring a management company.

7. You do not intend to be an employer: If you hire a resident manager or other employees to help manage your property, then you outright become an employer. You will have to take care of payroll as well as deal with a number of several legal requirements and considerations. However, since the company is an independent contractor, it avoids putting you in a position where you have to be an employer, and the hassles that come with it.

8. Your property is part of an affordable housing system: If you are a participant in an affordable housing system or program, things do tend to get complicated. In such programs, the property owner will receive financial aid that may come in the form of a grant, tax credits, or a low interest loan. In return, you agree to rent out at least a part of your property to tenants who earn below a certain threshold. To keep being privy to this financial aid, you, the proprietor, has to adhere to these stipulations.

The trouble is that even at face value, many such rules are complicated. There obviously will be a lot at stake here, and you may be unfamiliar with many of these things. In such a case, hiring a property management company with expertise and considerable experience with the housing system you adhere to will be worthwhile.

Conclusion

We have come to the end of the book. Thank you for reading and congratulations for reading until the end.

I hope this book was able to help you to understand how to invest in rental property and make great passive income year in year out.

The truth is; rental property ownership is almost never straightforward. You will have to consider factors such as time, neighborhood, unnecessarily problematic tenants, etc. However, now is a good time to be a property owner because house prices have fallen, which makes it easier for positive cash flow to be something you look forward to.

What you need to do is handle your property like a business and take seriously every facet of owning this business. If you follow the recommendations in this book, your rental business will create for you a steady stream of passive income.

The next step is to implement what you have learned.

PS: I'd like your feedback. If you are happy with this book, please leave a review on Amazon.

Please leave a review for this book on Amazon by visiting the page below:

https://amzn.to/2VMR5qr

www.ingramcontent.com/pod-product-compliance
Lightning Source LLC
Chambersburg PA
CBHW030516220526
45464CB00006B/2820